CHESHIR
150 YEARS AGO

A unique collection of views of Cheshire 1825-1840

Compiled by Frank Graham
From Old Prints

Original Publisher
FRANK GRAHAM

1991 EDITION

PRINTWISE PUBLICATIONS LIMITED
40-42 Willan Industrial Estate, Vere St, Salford M5 2GR
061-745 9168

Reprint organised, and additional material written by

Published 1991 by Printwise Publications Limited
47 Bradshaw Road, Tottington, Bury, Lancs BL8 3PW.

Warehouse & Orders:
40-42 Willan Ind. Estate, Vere Street (off Eccles New Road)
Salford M5 3GR
061 745 9168

Printed and bound by Manchester Free Press
Paragon Mill, Jersey Street, Manchester M4 6FP
061-236 8822

CHESHIRE 150 YEARS AGO

This is the latest offering in Printwise Publications' policy of re-printing old, rare and scarce books of local interest and making them available at reasonable prices.

I've enjoyed the searching and rummaging and am thankful for the help given by the second-hand book dealers all over Manchester and Lancashire. Being brought up in Widnes (while it was still in Lancashire), the first three books have covered Lancashire (Lancs Halls; Inns and Taverns; Curiosities) but now Widnes has been annexed to Cheshire it seems only fair to turn south to that county.

As Frank Graham says on the original introduction overleaf Cheshire in the 1800s has not been overwritten. There are now many volumes covering villages and towns of Cheshire in pictures, but prior to the camera only Chester seemed to attract the painters and artists. At last I came across this book at one of Bob Dobson's book fairs and I found it interesting and educational. After checking with book dealers that it was indeed hard to get hold of, getting permission to reprint from Frank and checking with Cheshire Libraries (the only copies left with them were falling to bits), I knew I'd found the next book.

Seeing the first copies I feel the printers have done a good job reproducing the prints — some seem clearer than the originals, one of the benefits of laser scanning. I hope you get as much enjoyment looking at Cheshire between 1830 and 1860 as I have had in bringing it to you.

Dedicated to Andrew & Lynne from MFP.
for their patience in getting the Book & the Quality just right.

ORIGINAL FOREWORD

In the following pages we present a picture of Cheshire in the first half of the nineteenth century. We have used almost one hundred old prints to show what the towns and villages of Cheshire were like in those days and have illustrated the castles and country houses when they were in a better state of preservation than they are today.

In the case of Chester we had plenty of prints to choose from, but in the rest of Cheshire there is a remarkable scarcity of old views. Thomas Allom's book—*The Counties of Chester, Derby, Nottingham, Leicester, Rutland and Lincoln*—published in 1839, has been very useful. In its day it was one of the most popular illustrated books of the area.

For Chester we have used J. Romney's *Chester and its Environs*, 1851, and J. S. Prout's *Antiquities of Chester* c. 1840, besides a large number of fine lithographs by G. Pickering and W. Tasker. These two artists in numerous drawings depicted the streets of Chester with great care and detail.

The prints by S. Hooper have been taken from the famous work of Francis Grose called *The Antiquities of England and Wales*, 1773-87. The views by E. Dayes are from John Aikin's *Description of the Country from Thirty to Forty miles round Manchester* published in 1795.

Many of the small views of mansions are from J. P. Neale's *Views of Seats of Noblemen and Gentlemen* published in parts from 1822 to 1829.

The remaining views are from a variety of sources. Most of the prints are reproduced in the same size as the originals, but a few have been slightly reduced.

Frank Graham

We must thank Frank Graham for kind permission to reproduce his fine book.

LIST OF PLATES

BRIDGE STREET, CHESTER.

OLD BRIDGE STREET, CHESTER.

BRIDGE STREET.

BRIDGE STREET, CHESTER.

LOWER BRIDGE STREET.

LOWER BRIDGE STREET, LOOKING DOWN.

BRIDGE STREET ROW, CHESTER.

BOFF. FALCON INN. HOME BREWD ALE
BOFF'S WINE & SPIRIT VAULTS
BRIDGE St
CHESTER

ROWS IN BRIDGE STREET, CHESTER.

LOWER BRIDGE STREET, CHESTER.

WATERGATE STREET, CHESTER.

WATERGATE STREET.
LOOKING UP

HOUSE IN WATERGATE STREET, CHESTER. DATE 1652, INSCRIBED "GOD'S PROVIDENCE IS MINE INHERITANCE."

"A picus remembrance of the owner; whose family, it is said, escaped the plague which raged in the neighbouring houses."

HOUSE S.SIDE OF WATERGATE STREET, CHESTER.

WATERGATE STREET ROW, CHESTER.

WATERGATE STREET, CHESTER.

NDON HOUSE 31
NA
WATER GATE ST CHESTER
J.S. Prout

EASTGATE STREET, CHESTER.

EASTGATE STREET.

THE CASTLE, and ST. BRIDGET'S CHURCH.

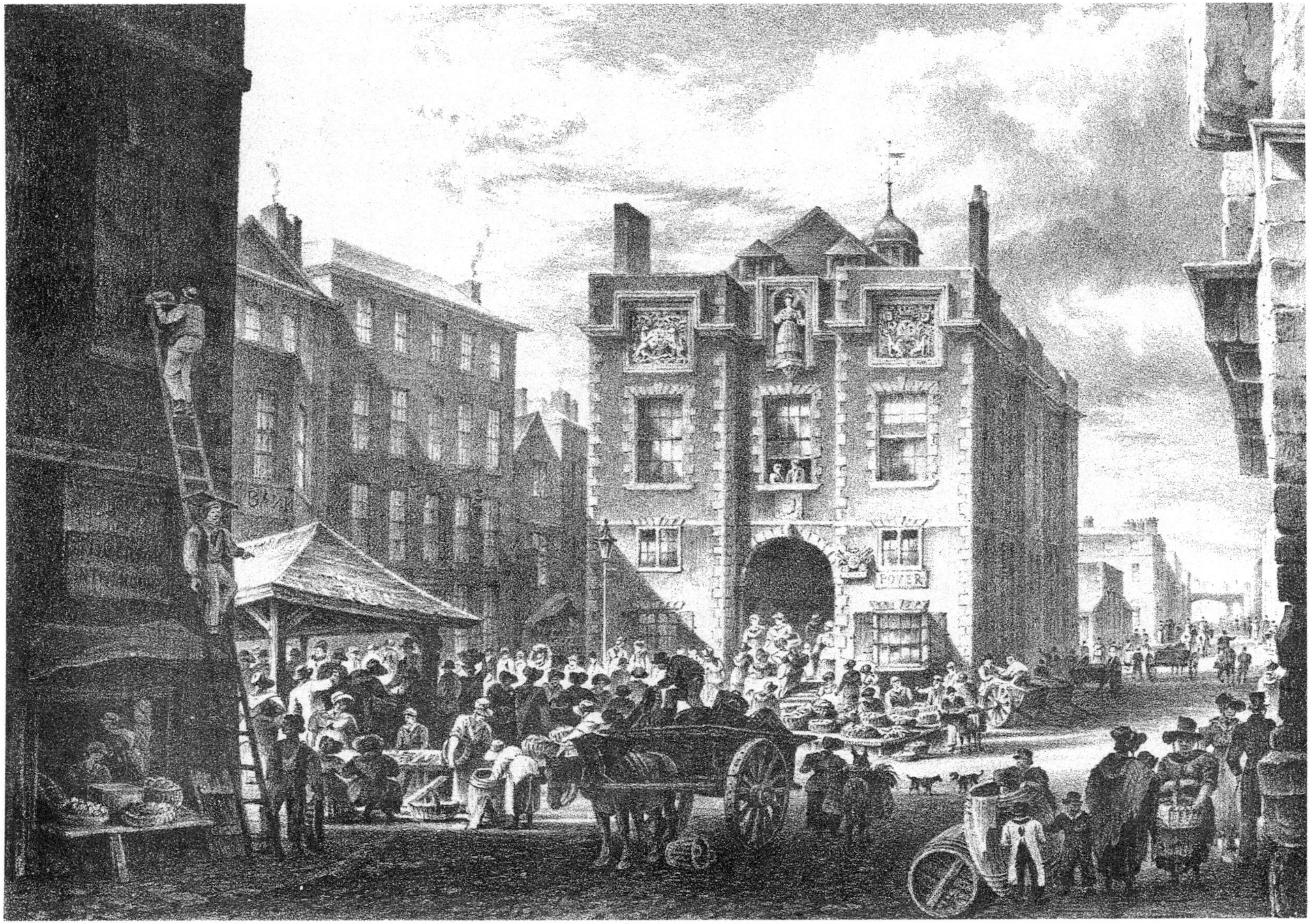

NORTHGATE STREET.
(EXCHANGE, FISH AND VEGETABLE MARKETS.)

NORTHGATE STREET, CHESTER.

NORTHGATE STREET.

THE OLD BRIDGE, HILL, PRISON, etc. CHESTER.

CHESTER BRIDGE.

THE NEW BRIDGE, CHESTER.

THE NEW or WATER TOWER CHESTER.

CHESTER, FROM HAND-BRIDGE.

WATER TOWER, FROM THE DEE BASIN, CHESTER.

VIEW FROM THE WALLS OF CHESTER — LOOKING INTO WALES.

WATER TOWER, CHESTER.
THE MUSEUM OF THE MECHANICS INSTITUTION.

VIEW OF HUGH LUPUS's HALL, AND THE EXCHEQUER IN CHESTER CASTLE

CHESTER CASTLE,

CHESTER CASTLE,

S.E. VIEW OF
THE CITY OF CHESTER

A PERSPECTIVE VIEW OF THE CATHEDRAL CHURCH OF CHESTER, IN CHESHIRE.

THE PHOENIX TOWER, CHESTER WALLS.

CHESTER.

LYME HALL. THE SEAT  OF THOMAS LEGH ESQ.

VIEW OF LIME HALL.

LYME HALL, CHESHIRE.

LYME HALL, CHESHIRE.

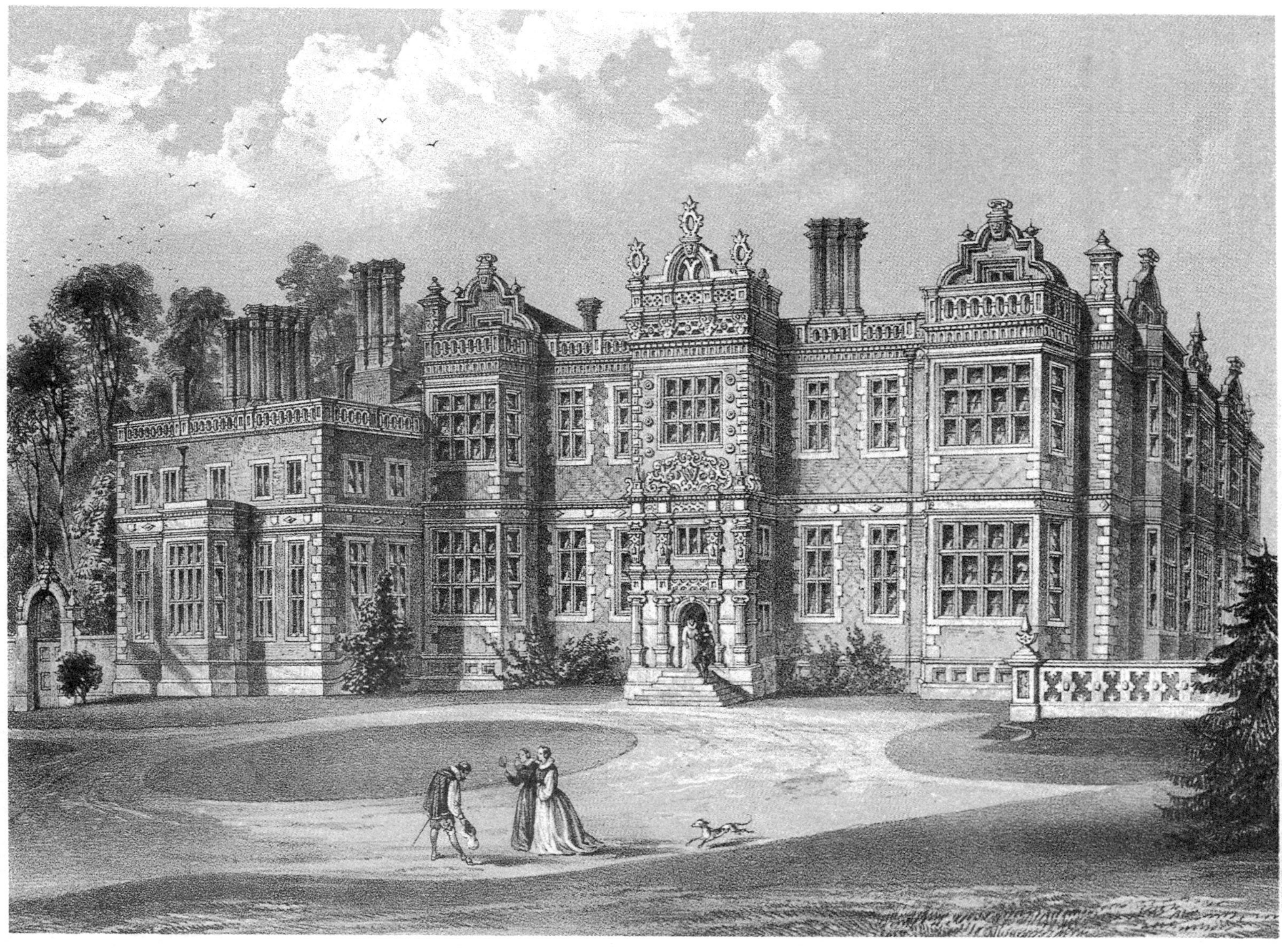

CREWE HALL. THE SEAT OF THE RIGHT HON. LORD CREWE

CREWE HALL, CHESHIRE.

VIEW OF MACCLESFIELD.

HATHERTON LODGE — Co CHESTER.

PROSPECT OF NANTWICH CHURCH IN CHESHIRE.

VIEW OF NANTWICH

THE OLD TOWN HALL, NANTWICH, CHESHIRE.

HIGH LEGH IN CHESHIRE, THE SEAT OF HENRY CORNWALL LEGH, ESQ^r.

CROSS AT SANDBACH

SANDBACH FREE GRAMMAR SCHOOL.

BIRKHEDDE PRIORY CHESHIRE.

MOTTRAM LONGDENDALE.

VIEW OF MOTTRAM CHURCH.

BEESTON CASTLE.

BEESTON CASTLE, CHESHIRE.

BEESTON CASTLE.

STOCKPORT.

VIEW OF STALEY HALL.

VIEW OF STALEY BRIDGE.

SOUTH-EAST VIEW OF LITTLE MORETON HALL, CHESHIRE.

VIEW OF THE SOUTH SIDE OF THE COURT OF LITTLE MORETON HALL, CHESHIRE.

VIEW OF DUKINFIELD HALL.

VIEW OF DUKINFIELD BRIDGE.

VIEW OF DUKINFIELD LODGE.

DUKINFIELD LODGE.
CHESHIRE.

BRERETON HALL.
CHESHIRE.

DORFOLD HALL.
THE SEAT OF Mrs TOMKINSON.

DE TABLEY PARK.

TABLEY HOUSE & CHAPEL.
CHESHIRE

THE COURT-YARD OF HOOTON HALL, CHESHIRE.

The ancient Seat of the Stanley Family, taken down in 1778

HOOTON HALL TAKEN DOWN 1778.

HOOTON IN CHESHIRE, THE SEAT OF SIR WM. STANLEY BART.

VALE ROYAL. THE SEAT OF 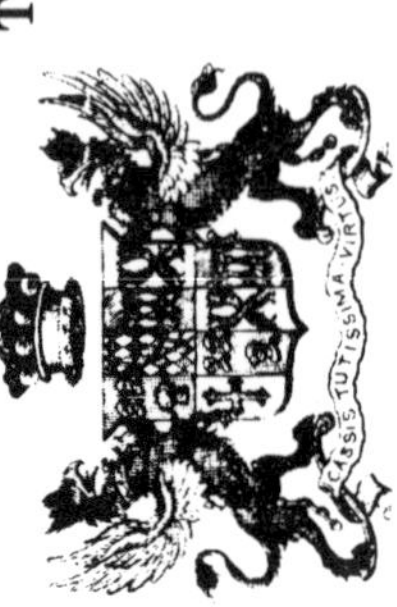 THE RIGHT HON LORD DELAMERE.

ANCIENT CASTLELLET IN DODDINGTON PARK, CHESHIRE.

CHOLMONDELEY CASTLE, CHESHIRE.

ENTRANCE  HALL.

CHOLMONDELEY CASTLE.

VIEW OF HYDE HALL.

VIEW OF POYNTON.

VIEW OF HARDEN HALL.

EAST FRONT OF EATON HALL, CHESHIRE.

WEST FRONT OF EATON HALL.

EATON HALL EAST FRONT.

CHESTER LODGE, ENTRANCE TO EATON PARK.

EATON HALL.

FARNDON.

BUNBURY CHURCH.

VIEW OF TATTON HALL.

RODE HALL.
CHESHIRE.

SOMERFORD BOOTHS HALL.
CHESHIRE.

COMBERMERE ABBEY.
CHESHIRE.

MARBURY HALL.
CHESHIRE.

SAIGHTON HALL.

TOFT HALL. CHESHIRE.

WEEVER HALL.

NEW BRIGHTON.